T0018714

PENGUIN BOOKS

Exploring Southeast Asia With Affandi: The Humanist Artist

Eva Wong Nava is an award-winning children's book author. She writes picture books to entertain, engage, and enthral young readers. She is also an art historian. When not writing for children, she meanders art museums and galleries waiting for the next piece of art work to speak to her and inspire another story. She weaves stories from art at *CarpeArte* Journal. When not writing, Eva teaches the art of picture book creation through her workshops under the brand, Picture Book Matters. Eva can be found on Twitter, Instagram and Facebook engaging people in conversations about art and stories.

Jeffrey Say is an art historian specialising in Singapore and Southeast Asian art history. Jeffrey has been instrumental in the development of art history studies at LASALLE College of the Arts, supporting artists to develop a contextual and historical understanding of the evolution of visual arts. In 2009, he designed the world's first Master's programme focussing on Asian modern and contemporary art histories. Jeffrey is a public advocate of the importance of art history to Singapore. He is a frequent public speaker at museums, universities and galleries, and conducts short courses which remain hugely popular among various publics. Jeffrey is also a regular commentator on the local visual arts scene. An author of numerous essays on art, his seminal co- edited work *Histories, Practices, Interventions: A Reader in Singapore Contemporary Art* (2016) remains a critical anthology for researchers, curators and students on Singapore art to date.

Quek Hong Shin is a Singaporean freelance author and illustrator whose works include picture books like *The Amazing Sarong, The Brilliant Oil Lamp and Universe of Feelings. The Incredible Basket*, was the winner of Best Children's Book at the 2019 Singapore Book Awards. He is also the illustrator for other children's titles like *The One and Only Inuka* and the *Ahoy, Navy!* series that was published in celebration of the Republic of Singapore Navy's 50th Anniversary in 2017.

PENGUIN BOOKS

USA | Canada | UK | Ireland | Australia
New Zealand | India | South Africa | China | Southeast Asia

Penguin Books is part of the Penguin Random House group
of companies whose addresses can be found at global.
penguinrandomhouse.com

Published by Penguin Random House SEA Pte Ltd
9, Changi South Street 3, Level 08-01,
Singapore 486361

Penguin
Random House
SEA

First published in Penguin Books by Penguin Random House
SEA 2022

ISBN 9789814954389

www.penguin.sg

EXPLORING SOUTHEAST ASIA WITH

AFFANDI

THE HUMANIST ARTIST

Eva Wong Nava and Jeffrey Say

Illustrated by Quek Hong Shin

PENGUIN BOOKS

An imprint of Penguin Random House

This is a story of a man who taught himself how to make art. This is a story of an Indonesian man whose heart was filled with love for the everyday man and woman that he felt compelled to paint them. This is a story of a man whose style became a representation of modern Indonesian art.

4

This artist was named Affandi.

And his story has roots in India. By the time he went to live in India, Affandi was forty-two years old and already knew how to paint. A scholarship made it possible for him to study more about art-making at an academy there. But Affandi used that money to travel around India instead. While travelling for two years, he observed the people, the environment, and landscape. He was touched by what he saw. Most of all, he was affected by the sight of homeless people scattered around the towns and lining the sidewalks.

8

When he returned to Cirebon,
his hometown in West Java,
he began a series of paintings
inspired by his travels in India.

*I will paint the people
who touched my life.*

He painted in the traditional way—
with brushes, stroking oil paint on
the canvas, creating dashes, dabs,
swirls, and whirls that made up
shapes of people.

But something happened that
changed the way he was to paint.

Affandi watched in dismay as his paint brush snapped in two. Why didn't he think to bring another one?

How can I paint now with no brush? What would other painters do? What would be a painter's tool besides a paint brush?

These questions tumbled around Affandi's head as he looked at the rollicking countryside of West Java that spread before him. There was such beauty, but at the same time, it was not an ideal kind of beauty. There was a wildness that he wanted to capture.

Affandi knew that he needed to be honest with his art. He knew that he had to paint from his heart. Only then would he be an authentic artist.

By this time, Affandi had been an artist for more than twenty years. He had always painted with a brush.

So, without a paint brush, Affandi was helpless.

His brows furrowed in anxiety.
His heart beat in anguish.
His fingers trembled in despair.

But without a tool for painting, he stared helplessly at the flowers and trees before him.

Looking at his hands gave Affandi an idea.
He wiggled his fingers.

He stuck his right index finger out and waved it
from side to side, like a wiper swiping away the
rain drops on a car's wind screen.

He dabbed this finger with some paint and made a
swerve on the canvas.

What if...

My fingers became my brush?

His hands shook with excitement.

17

Some artists he knew were obsessed
with only painting beautiful sceneries
and people. That was not what Affandi
wanted to do.

What if...

I question the idea of beauty?

Squeezing paint
from its tube,
Affandi plastered
his canvas with
dollops of colours.

His head filled with whirls of ideas.

What if...

My thumbs knew what to do?

His thumbs fidgeted with excitement.
His fingers twitched in anticipation.

Affandi lifted his hand and a magical sensation spread through him. As if in a trance, he smeared the dollops of colours and smudged them on the canvas with his thumbs.

He worked hard to make patterns on the canvas. He worked hard to make these patterns into lines and shapes that the human eye could recognize.

Taking a walk along the coast one day,
someone caught Affandi's eye. The beggar
was on his knees, a begging bowl in front of him.
Affandi's heart ached with sorrow for this man.

What if...

I let my emotions
do the painting?

The only way he could capture his feelings
was to paint this man and his suffering.

Sweat beaded on his brows and upper lips.

He squeezed more paint from the tubes.

He made more lines with his fingers and additional shapes with his thumbs.

He created furiously, urgently, and energetically. . . until

24

. . . a picture of a man formed instinctively on the canvas.

'Ahhh! The painting is finished,' he said with a sigh.
Affandi always knew when the work was done: it was the
moment when he felt the highs of his emotions falling.

Affandi worked hard in expressing his feelings for
the people and places he saw with his very own
eyes, using his fingers and thumbs to paint.

25

This is the story of Affandi, the artist with a human touch. This is the story of an Indonesian artist with a big dose of empathy. Touched by the people he observed and came to love he painted all their stories, dignifying them with his art that came from his heart.

Who was Affandi?

Affandi (1907–1990) was born in Cirebon in West Java, Indonesia. Affandi did not have any formal art training. He taught himself to paint at the age of twenty-seven and learned from reproductions of Western artists that he saw in the copies of *Studio*, an art magazine from London. Affandi had a unique painting style in which he would squeeze the paint directly from the tube and use energetic lines and non-naturalistic colours, giving his works an expressionistic quality. He preferred to paint subjects that reflect the realities of Indonesian life such as an old woman, a beggar and cock fighting rather than beautiful landscapes. He was the first modern artist in Southeast Asia to achieve international recognition. After receiving a grant from the Indian government, Affandi was in India from 1949 to 1951, where he studied at the renowned institution of higher learning Visva Bharati, Santineketan in West Bengal, founded by the Indian Nobel Laureate Rabindranath Tagore. From there, Affandi went to Europe and exhibited his works in major cities such as Paris, London, and Rome. He also visited the United States, where he was made Honorary Professor of Painting at Ohio State University. Affandi participated in major biennials in Brazil (1952), Venice (1954), and Sao Paulo (1956). In 1974, he received an honorary doctorate from the University of Singapore.

Affandi
Self-Portrait
1975
Oil on canvas, 130 x 100.5 cm
Gift of the artist
Collection of National Gallery Singapore

© Affandi Foundation
Image courtesy of National Heritage Board, Singapore

Affandi painted this in 1975. By then, he was almost seventy years old. Self-portraits are a common subject matter for many artists. Affandi painted many self-portraits.

Let's Talk About the Artwork

1. This is a self-portrait of Affandi. Why do you think artists painted themselves?
2. What colours stand out in this painting? What effects do those colours have on the painting?
3. The picture is created primarily from lines. What types of lines did Affandi use for the different features of the face?
4. How would you describe the expression on the face of the artist? What effect does it have on you?
5. It is known that Affandi painted by squeezing the paint directly from the tube. Do you see any evidence of that in the painting?